Gorgeous Inside

FROM DEALING
TO HEALING

BY PALOMA FREEMAN

Cover design by Leah Quinn

Author photo by Lafa Britto, Lafayette Britto Photography

Editing and formatting by ChristianEditingServices.com; Jen Miller, editor.

Dedicated to:

God

Undoubtedly, my greatest thank you is submitted humbly to my Father above. Your strength has carried me when I couldn't walk. Your love has fortified every scar for purpose. Thank You for keeping me in the palm of Your hand when I didn't even want to be part of the body. Thank You for loving me with a love so pure. I pray that all of You, and none of me, is glorified through my testimony. I pray that Your Holy Spirit will penetrate those You've ordained to receive the words herein, just as an encounter with You changed my entire life.

My Husband

I could not have done this without you. Many times I wanted to shut down or give up baring my heart in print and you repeatedly spoke life over my purpose. You didn't just speak to the current me, you encouraged the future me. I count it an honor to be your wife and best friend. Your prayers and your love make me brave and unapologetically unashamed. This one is for you, my king. I love you forever.

Madre

You are my heart. Thank you for supporting me through this process. Thank you for planting countless seeds in my life. You are the most beautiful woman I've known. Your selflessness moves me daily. I pray this book inspires you to live limitlessly and step out in faith with no parachute, like never before.

My Midwives

From the texts and calls that were Holy Spirit led, to the women who were obedient enough to encourage me when I didn't believe in myself, to the store owner who asked for my autograph, and to my editor: thank you. You each have played an intricate role in this pregnant journey. By the beauty of the Holy Spirit inside you, I delivered this book at full term. By your love, I did not abort the mission. I really can't thank you ladies enough. I pray that I have served as a midwife in birthing your dreams as well. Let's hold hands and go!

Table of Contents

Why This Book Is for Every Woman 7

1. Lose the Noose 11

2. Fakin' It to Faithin' It 19

3. Turning Scars into Stars 25

4. From Dealing to Healing 33

5. The Dance 37

6. Giftwrapped for God 53

7. No New Friends? 61

8. Staying in Your Own Lane 67

9. On the Verge of Your Merge 73

10. Becoming Your Own Stepping Stone 75

11. Birthing a Blessing 79

12. Gorgeous Inside: Birthing Base, Balance, and Beauty 93

The Gorgeous Inside Challenge 97

Why This Book Is for Every Woman

What if I told you that every orchestrated attack by the enemy is part of God's plan to redirect your pain into purpose? How many times have you found yourself in tears as you cried out, *why*? Can you recall? How many tears have you held back? How many attitudes did you catch? How much guilt have you carried? How many times have you blocked out all emotion, as I did, because to *feel* meant the pain was real, and you just didn't want to deal with that heartache?

Although we haven't walked in the exact same shoes, I can bet we've all fallen and been hurt at one time or another. In a world that celebrates the "bad bitch," this book honors the inner-beauty queens. In a world that says, "you can't turn a hoe into a housewife," and "people don't change," this book is to remind you that God can turn any submitted heart into whomever He desires for His purpose.

When the rain falls, it just makes our roots grow deeper. As the tests come, they remind us that scars aren't to be covered up; they're to be uncovered so God can do the healing and create beauty from ashes! (Isaiah 61:3)

As I wrote this book, I thought back on every obstacle that tried to take me out. At first, I didn't want you to read those. I could have lied to you instead, by telling you that pressing forward to healing and freedom is easy. But, honestly, writing this book with vulnerability has been by far the most challenging spiritual directive of my life. But as I pressed forward, I wanted you— my sister in Christ—to press with me "in spirit and in truth" (John 4:24). Our stories may be different, but our invaluable substance of spirit is meant to be the same.

As a young adult I watched the movie *8 Mile*. Although I wouldn't be so inclined to watch it today, due to personal conviction, it taught me an unforgettable, powerful lesson. The main character is an aspiring rapper from the projects. He had all the odds stacked against him. Even though he knew he was gifted, he struggled with stage fright. He battled so much fire in order to walk in his purpose.

When he had a large battle performance, he knew his opponent would go for the jugular with rival rhymes and try to cut him open where it would most hurt, and force bleed all his insecurities. Before the opponent got that chance, the aspiring rapper performed first—and told on himself through his own lyrics. He said everything his opponent could have possibly said. When it was time for his opponent to flow, the rival was silent.

When we know our enemy's war tactics, we have an edge to learn how to fight to win. Although the movie example entails a battle in human form, we know from the apostle Paul that our battle is not against flesh and blood, but a spiritual battle (Ephesians 6:12).

Regardless of how you've been wounded in life, *Gorgeous Inside* demonstrates that every single attack in your life is strategic, and explains how you can meet each one with power, humility, and inner beauty.

There's freedom and priceless value in our individual, unique testimonies. Allow mine, through this book, to also show you how to reach for your sister's hand and help her press through her pain in order to live in her purpose and authentic beauty too.

Chapter One
LOSE THE NOOSE

We feel such empathy for the child that we hear was abused or otherwise wounded in some way. We cringe at the mere thought of the animal who committed such an atrocity. The dire truth is that many deeply-wounded children grow into older versions of those we once felt compassion for. There's healing for some, yet others undertake the daily chore of masking how they truly feel. Whether from abuse, abandonment, loss, or other deep wounding, the constant act of veiling the emotional aftermath is a heavy coping mechanism.

Imagine your toes having just enough strength and space to lift the weight of your body as a noose gradually pulls tighter and tighter around your neck. Sure, you're breathing, but under what conditions? The residual outcome of deep wounds to the spirit feels like asphyxiation; it has a way of making you feel as if you're choking. But because there's just enough air to breathe, you're convinced you must endure it. You carry that weight on your shoulders through life, everywhere you go, and drag it into everything you do. It's *heavy*.

You've likely asked yourself how anyone could have allowed such pain to you as a child. Just the thought of someone hurting you to such an extent—likely someone you thought you knew and could trust—weighs a ton inside you.

> *As a child, I remained silent for many years.*
> *I also tried to apply false memory syndrome to*
> *my experiences—a term I didn't know until I was*
> *grown. My noose was abuse. I thought perhaps*
> *I had imagined the abuse, perhaps conjured*
> *recollections that never actually occurred. I tried*
> *to convince myself that my memories were like a*
> *boogeyman under the bed; they didn't really exist.*
> *I even formed the idea that I must have somehow*
> *created the memories. As an adult, though, I*
> *began to see with more clarity the truth in my*
> *memories, and I could no longer pawn them off*
> *as imagination. In truth, I had been abused.*

Many times we construct lies that lessen the hurt of reality. Studies have proven that when the truth is too painful to bear, it's quite conceivable to build fabrications that are easier to manage psychologically and emotionally. For a young child, protective fabrications are typically not difficult to create. After all, the "bad stuff" often looks and feels like monsters and nightmares.

You must understand that you do not walk this path alone, that your victimization was *not* your fault, and you do not have to remain silent, bound in your spirit by the noose of abuse that's cutting off the oxygen to your spirit. You do not have to allow *any* past travesties to wither your present and future relationships. You do not have to be bound from your purpose, with pain wrapped around your neck. Neither do you have to allow adversities of the past to afflict and overtake your attitude one more day. You can be freed—starting today.

Start by owning the fact that your past wounding is authentic, and stop ignoring that it happened. Time moves forward, not backward, so you must also accept that the past cannot be altered or erased. Acknowledging the reality of your victimization will allow you to truly heal once and for all. Whether physical, mental, sexual, or spiritual, you must cut the noose of abuse today. Now is the time to make the decision to release any venom that was spewed your way and replace it with nourishment for your healing and growth.

Walk with me and the Lord through this book. Let me take your hand and show you how you can become free of past pain and fully embrace God's best for your future. You have the power to transform anything negative in your life into positive resolution.

> For the Spirit God gave us does not make us timid, but gives us power, love and self-discipline.
> — 2 TIMOTHY 1:7

> Be transformed by the renewing of your mind.
> — ROMANS 12:2

This journey will not be easy, but it will be worth it. Bear with me as we bare it all to the Lord. Show your true self—no mask, no pretense, no Photoshop, and no filters. I cannot stand to see one more sister walking dead!

You may be asking yourself, *Why is it anyone's business what I've been through? Why should I bare it all to the Lord?*

The journey to inner freedom is not necessarily about sharing your scars with anyone prematurely, but about giving God your hurts at the first sign of puncture. It's about revisiting places of hurt within you, and addressing and healing the new ones as they arise. Life comes with adversities against each of us, but no one can do the internal work for you. In photos, for example, we have the tools to be able to adjust the lighting, fix our blemishes, and crop out whatever we want without a second thought. In life, though, we must choose the Light—Jesus Christ—be the Light, and fight for God's light and healing within us *daily*. There are things we may attempt to crop out, but in reality those are oftentimes only a fraction of what we've accumulated through the years that we have yet to deal with.

> The journey to inner freedom is not necessarily about sharing your scars with anyone prematurely, but about giving God your hurts at the first sign of puncture.

Remember that a glow stick must be broken before it can shine. For us, Christ broke the seal, giving us an opportunity to see heaven's light. Do not skip the hard work in allowing God to perfect us. This requires us to surrender ourselves into His hands repeatedly.

Healing occurs when we expose our brokenness, let God's healing light shine on our cuts, and give Him the glory in the beginning, middle, and end of our story. Our scars can represent *beautiful stories* that reflect our purpose:

> The Spirit of the Sovereign LORD is on me, because the LORD has anointed me to proclaim good news to the poor. He has sent me to bind up the brokenhearted, to proclaim freedom for the captives and release from darkness for the prisoners, to

> proclaim the year of the LORD's favor and the day of
> vengeance of our God, to comfort all who mourn,
> and provide for those who grieve in Zion— to
> bestow on them a crown of beauty instead of ashes,
> the oil of joy instead of mourning, and a garment
> of praise instead of a spirit of despair. They will be
> called oaks of righteousness, a planting of the LORD
> for the display of his splendor.
>
> — ISAIAH 61:1-3

Perhaps you were not abused or otherwise deeply wounded. If you're saying truthfully to yourself, *I've never experienced any form of wounding; I had a great upbringing; my life's been pretty smooth,* that's awesome. You're truly blessed. However, your best friend or your hater might have personal experiences filled with hurt, and you have a responsibility as a believer (and a human being) to not only inspire and empower others but also to work to understand others beyond their layers of makeup and designer stilettos. Our understanding must reach beyond the healthy fit lifestyles, Twitter followers, Instagram selfies, and other images we let the world see.

Think about it: Few people expose in social media the depth of their depression, photos of their teary, saddened eyes, or self-inflicted scars from suicide attempts. My point is not whether we should post our pain to the world; my point is simply a reminder that even though pictures are worth a thousand words, they *still* have the capability to withhold the whole truth.

It's also important to remember to never compare your portion with that of another's portion. Someone may appear to have it all together, but the truth is that you have no idea about the battles others are going through, and the tests they've passed to maintain their outward posture—regardless of how well you think you know someone.

How much do you *really* know about those in your life? Without knowledge of another person's needs, there is no determination toward extending help. Once you know that someone near you is silently crying out for empathy and healing, you can ask yourself what you can do to help.

> *He placed the crack pipe in my mouth. When I revealed to my stepfather that I had smoked weed, I had no idea he would use that admission as an opportunity to pressure me into consuming crack, such a destructive poison. After previously rejecting him from our lives for some time, I had finally opened up to him, and he used that moment, my vulnerability and trust, to manipulate me.*
>
> *Conversely, he had played an instrumental part in restoring our involvement in church, and he loved my mama and provided financial stability for our family. Naturally, I thought I could trust him. But then he trapped me in that unwanted secret. I felt guilty because he knew my dirt. For a year he used that information to his advantage.*
>
> *His manipulation came in many forms: from bribing me to ride along on his drug pick-ups, as a condition for providing me a ride to the mall, to telling me it would break my mama's heart if she knew of his addiction—and my drug use.*
>
> *Not long after his addiction and mental disorders worsened, his bipolar episodes brought physical abuse at my expense. Whenever*

my mama was away from home, he found opportunities to mistreat me. I knew it was only a matter of time before the abuse grew more severe.

On the surface, my academics were declining, I was getting into fights and altercations with my peers, and I had a disrespectful attitude toward authority. Underneath it all, no one knew what I was returning home to face at the end of each day.

Everyone has a story. Even if you don't understand another's actions, take a moment to look beneath the surface. What you might view as erroneous behavior may actually be a despairing cry for help.

Inside, I was screaming.

17

When you pass through the waters, I will be with you;
and through the rivers, they shall not overwhelm you;
when you walk through fire you shall not be burned,
and the flame shall not consume you.

— Isaiah 43:2

Chapter Two
FAKIN' IT
TO FAITHIN' IT

" **F**ake it 'til you make it." This is a common phrase used to inspire people to conduct themselves as if they'd already achieved their intended goals. However, there are flaws to this colloquialism. While I absolutely agree in the power of speaking aspirations into existence, there is a problem with the term "fake it." Faking it can become toxic because it forces an individual to maintain a lie. How exhausting is that?! To maintain falsehood you have to become a phony version of yourself. Instead, I urge you to "faith it."

Hebrews 11:1 states that "faith is being sure of what we hope for and certain of what we do not see." The concept of having faith is determined by identifying and believing in a purpose. When you practice and exhibit true faith, your entire essence says, "I have a purpose to fulfill and I am not doing it to impress others. I'm doing it because it's what I'm *called* to do." When you have faith, you don't have to fake it; you just have to choose to ignite it daily.

Many of us have placed temporary Band-Aids where God should be the permanent restorer. We've attempted to cover and conceal the hurt and fragmented areas of our hearts and lives in order to withstand another day. As a result, there are so many broken beauties walking around, living in counterfeit contentment. The walking dead are deceptively beautiful. Many are affluent, and all are of varying ethnicities and backgrounds.

> Hurt has no biases, but how we deal with it is always a choice.

Hurt has *no biases,* but how we deal with it is always a *choice.*

The idolatry that afflicts contemporary society is real. The hurting, the broken, the emotionally and spiritually needy, and the seemingly "put together" are running to temporary fixes to pacify themselves into believing they're happy. They're running to romantic relationships, retail shopping, drugs and alcohol, and countless other superficial ends that mimic satisfaction and fulfillment, and then quickly dissipate.

> *For years I attempted to sooth myself. Somewhere in a room full of loud music and social status I spiraled out of control. On the mere surface it appeared I had overcome the Goliaths of my past. I was thriving in college (something others said I would never be able to accomplish), and I was earning a stable income and working on becoming more physically fit. My exterior was solidly intact and full of composure. The problem was rooted in what could not be seen by the naked eye.*
>
> *Inside, my roaring spirit would not be quiet, no matter how many accomplishments or layers of facades I piled on top of each other. I*

felt pressed to keep moving; I couldn't swallow staying stagnant. Not because I had a ton of deadlines and demands but because I couldn't stand the stillness and silence. It was in stillness and silence that I faced confronting my actions, my self-defeating thoughts, my ugly past and present, and what might be my future.

One night I lay in bed, feeling low after having sex with a "friend." How had I been able to hand over such a precious part of me, so freely, under the context of mere friendship? When had I convinced myself it was acceptable to have a "friend with benefits?"

Somewhere along the way I had rationalized casual sex as being perfectly okay. After all, it was just fun, right? We were two consensual adults, right? These were the questions I asked myself in the darkness to justify the self-destructive actions I had allowed myself to commit.

Something profound happens when we try to remove the pen of life from God's hands. We get humbled.

The bed of fun under the silken sheets of casual sex where I lay that night awakened me to see how devalued, how thoughtless, how inconsequential, how ungrateful I had become. I had unmade God's intricately designed and woven, one-of-kind, beautiful, priceless, irreplaceable human life—mine. And not only mine but also the other priceless human I had been casually engaging with immorally, whose spirit I was participating in defacing.

Can you relate? Do you have a friend you always resort to calling to fulfill your worldly needs? What about a "boo" you tend to text, or a drug you reach for when you aim to satisfy your impulses? Do you get offended at correction? Do you crave attention and submit to "likes" from your peers for affirmation? Do you define your status through your social climb or the public view that others have of you? Do you belong to cliques and circles that are built on nothing more than trivial commonalities?

All is not lost. There is redeemable hope!

It's in the scope of such background battles that true victory can prevail. But we cannot afford to fight our battles with flesh and blood, "for our struggle is not against flesh and blood, but against the rulers, against the authorities, against the powers of this dark world and against the spiritual forces of evil in the heavenly realms" (Ephesians 6:12). The battle must be fought with our *spirits*—in prayer, in feeding on the living Word of God, and in worship to our Creator

> *I cried my heart out. I felt as if I were dying because, truthfully, I was laying a part of myself to rest. The Apostle Paul said it like this: "Put to death the misdeeds of the body" (Romans 8:13). The part of me that called on my peers and superficial outlets had to be put to death and buried in order to bring forth the humble part of me that could authentically kneel before God's throne of grace, mercy, and redemption. There was only One who could answer my call: His Son, Jesus, who died so I could truly live freely in my spirit.*
>
> *I was done faking it.*

Let's be clear; there's nothing wrong with looking nice, investing in yourself, courting romantic interests, or having friends to socialize with. However, anything can become problematic when you use such channels as your primary outlets to fulfil the needs of your spirit.

Circumstances transform into issues when the complimentary becomes supplementary.

When going a day without trivial things actually flexes your attitude, it's time for a real change. With faith and healing you find comfort and contentment in being transparent. Although you may have awareness about the road that still stretches ahead, and recognize that you've not yet reached the finish line, it's at this level of trust in God and who He created you to be that you must take authority to carry out your healing and your ordained task. You must die to self in order to undertake the process of healing, so there's no further need to be artificial. It's in complete healing that you no longer have to "fake it." You move with the will of God, not with your own, nor with your moods and addictions, and certainly not with the actions and judgments of others.

> Circumstances transform into issues when the complimentary becomes supplementary.

Everything fades with the wind. We live in a fickle world, one in which people say one thing but do another. With changing philosophies, climates, and societal standards, nothing appears to be set in stone. However, you must have a firm allegiance to your faith—a steel rod of determination running through you that holds your spiritual spine straight to stand strong and immovable.

Trusting God with your entire heart is not just a cute idiom to be printed on a stylish T-shirt. Faith is a fidelity that requires purposeful dedication and unwavering commitment. Having faith is no "cop-out," as some unbelievers will say. In a world that attempts to present you with a million reasons to discard faith, truly possessing faith is an act of courage. At a place of "faithin' it," there's no need to fake anything. You manage your healing and ordained tasks with real accountability and a deep reverence for God.

In our humility we find God's empowerment.

Chapter Three
TURNING SCARS INTO STARS

There is a time for everything,
   and a season for every activity under the heavens:

a time to be born and a time to die,
   a time to plant and a time to uproot,
a time to kill and a time to heal,
   a time to tear down and a time to build,
a time to weep and a time to laugh,
   a time to mourn and a time to dance,
a time to scatter stones and a time to gather them,
   a time to embrace and a time to refrain from embracing,
a time to search and a time to give up,
   a time to keep and a time to throw away,
a time to tear and a time to mend,
   a time to be silent and a time to speak,
a time to love and a time to hate,
   a time for war and a time for peace.

— ECCLESIASTES 3:108

At some point in your journey, you must come to terms with your baggage—your scars—as well as updating your flight information—where you're headed in life.

As humans, we often attempt to grab old baggage with outdated journey information. Meanwhile, we may be missing a fundamental flight because we've over-packed for what was intended as a weekend vacation.

Imagine carrying the same old baggage full of unchanged and unwashed clothes everywhere you travel. Imagine wearing those same dirty clothes over and over. Not only would you collect a lot of stains, but you and your baggage wouldn't smell nice. It's not a matter of *if* there will be a stench; it's a matter of when. You would be carrying bacteria and disease-building germs that will infect you and all those around you.

> Yesterday's laundry is not today's business suit for success.

As Ecclesiastes 3:1 reminds us, there is a season for everything under the sun. New seasons require new luggage—a new attitude and expectations toward growth. Both should be labeled the same: Jesus Christ.

While you have likely sustained some self-inflicted injuries, some wounds were not your fault and not by your choice. Either way, those lessons were not meant to lessen you, God uses all wounding experiences to equip you and prune you to function at a level He preordained and designed you to operate at. The idea is to set your sights forward, not constantly gazing over your shoulder at past mistakes and misfortunes. You must learn to start each day *fresh*. After all, God said His mercies for you are "new every morning" (Lamentations 3:23). Each moment is a new opportunity, not only to forgive others but also to forgive and renew yourself.

GRUDGES ARE CONTAMINANTS

Do not allow others' toxic baggage to get mixed up with your own. A toxic person will pollute you. Some of the toxic clothes in your daily travel bag are your grudges against others. Carrying that baggage expends more energy than it takes to forgive those who have hurt you. Just as toxic is the resentments you've packed in your bag. Ponder the amount of energy it entails to avoid and loathe someone. The moments spent eluding conversation and giving the cold shoulder are far more time-consuming for you than for your offender. These are heavy weights you're choosing to add to your bag and carry around throughout your days. Aren't there far more important suits for success you need to pack in order to maximize your God-given time and energy?

Forgiveness does not imply that you must hold hands and sing "Kumbaya" with everyone who has ever wronged you. Forgiveness does not mean you have to invite the accused to your birthday party or to be your Facebook friend. **The hater should not be your motivator**. Not everyone needs to take a seat in the front row of your life. Sometimes it's necessary to love from the balcony.

HEALING TO HAPPINESS

When deep scars stop bleeding, you're no longer in a state of shock. If you can trust a doctor enough to bandage your wounds, and a pilot to land you safely, without ever questioning their credentials, why can't you trust God enough to do the same for you? **Stop handing people the keys to your happiness**. They'll infect and crash you every time. Not because they necessarily aim to disappoint or hurt you, but simply because they're human.

What do you say to the child in you who's been abused or neglected? Of course that's a rhetorical question, for what can possibly be said when the one person who was supposed to have protected you hurt you? I could feed you a plethora of possible explanations or give you the rationale that the abuse stems from the abuser's childhood. I could explain how an offender of that magnitude is preconditioned to bleed onto others from their unhealed scars. I could deduce the abuser's psyche all day—all the toxic baggage an abuser carries—but I won't. You must know that **sometimes there is no logical explanation, but there is always a spiritual explanation.**

LET IT GO

It's time to heal and move on to happiness. Paul said it best: "I do not consider myself yet to have taken hold of it. But one thing I do: Forgetting what is behind and straining toward what is ahead" (Philippians 3:13).

> *When my stepfather finally fled, I held on to some things: the social security card he accidentally left behind—and vengeance. I said to myself, one day, when I'm strong enough, I will get him back. I held on to this idea and mentally strategized how I would gain retribution for how he had wronged me. But the more time and energy I invested in thinking of revenge, the more I decapitated myself and my relationships.*
>
> *I began to read and study about the power of forgiveness.*
>
> *I immersed myself in God's Word on my own, instead of waiting for others to "feed me."*

His Word became my sustenance and I hungered for it daily.

Little by little, God began to peel off the layers of my heart—and oh how I cried. But when my eyes were dried, I made the conscious decision to no longer cry over the same things again. Once I had mourned my misfortunes and pain, I released them. It was a choice.

Change is a choice that makes us free.

Having released that unnecessary weight, I graduated to an elevated level of freedom. My freedom was solidified on a college field trip. We were visiting a local jail to gain a close perspective of Florida's criminal justice system. As we walked by the inmates, it dawned on me that in my juvenile years I could have very well been in the same shoes as one of them. I put my head down in shame as I felt no sense of entitlement. I was filled with complete and utter compassion.

When I looked up, there he was, on the other side of the bars. My abuser. The moment for verbal revenge that I had waited for had unexpectedly manifested. But out of the new, soft place of empathy, all I could do was smile at him—the kind of gentle smile that is birthed from agape love and grace. Instead of feeling vengeful and rage, and wanting to inflict pain on him the way he had on me, I felt my heart grasp hold of the sturdy dowel of compassion from which the flag of forgiveness gently waved. I wanted to hug him.

I'll honestly never know if my stepfather was lucid enough in that holding cell to realize it was me, but I knew God was faithful enough to set us both free.

As for my biological dad, it's difficult to describe him through the lens of my childhood. He and my mother divorced when I was four years old. So he, and my relationship with him, had been very inconsistent back then.

What I do remember from my childhood is waiting by a window, watching for him, and him not showing up at times. When he was present with me, it was evident that his love for me ran as deep as the ocean, but once we parted, there would be for long periods with no communication. He was my summer vacation dad exemplified—one season with him and in the off-season I'd long for his attention.

Longing for a consistent father figure is what kept me in hunger for the affection of others. I chased romantic relationships with the unconscious need for someone to fill the void my dad should have filled. This pattern was my normal. Just enough love here; just enough love there; just enough love to keep me silent enough not to complain, not to confront; just enough to keep me returning to the casual counterfeit of true, committed, covenant love. It was just enough to feed my ravenous hunger with temporary satisfaction. My hurt was evident in my actions, even though I rarely said anything about the real issue.

> It's our hearts that will always, eventually, give us away, revealing the truths we want to deny and hide.

I had grown to view my dad with such distrust and animosity that I became rude and disrespectful to him. I blamed him for a lot of my personal pain. But, at the end of the day, it wasn't him I was mad at. I was mad at myself for daily choosing the gown of bitterness as my expired attire. Each day I chose to pick up old baggage filled with the clothes of toxicity.

What I wasn't aware of in those early adult years was that God had already prepared for me a great banquet of deeply nurturing, filling, satisfying, forever-faithful love from the bounty of His incomprehensible love.

I pray that you, being rooted and established in love, may have power, together with all the Lord's holy people, to grasp how wide and long and high and deep is the love of Christ, and to know this love that surpasses knowledge—that you may be filled to the measure of all the fullness of God.

— Ephesians 3:17-19

When I forgave myself for everything toxic I was choosing each day to carry, God graced me to forgive others, including my dad. Realistically, how could I have expected anyone to view me with new eyes when I hadn't been doing the same for myself and others?

31

My dad developed a relationship with Christ in my early twenties and I see the fruit in his life. When I'm with him, I experience joy, laughter, and most of all freedom of heart and mind. I now see him through a new lens, as the new creature he is in Christ.

If it wasn't for my relationship with Christ, I know I would be the walking dead, heavily weighed down by the anger, comparison, defense, mistrust, longing, and lack of fulfillment I daily chose. Without grace and forgiveness, I know I wouldn't have the beautiful blended family I have today. I know I wouldn't be with the most loving man I'm blessed to call my husband. Had it not been for Christ, and for my willingness to have Him search my heart and reveal to me my expired attire that filled the closet and luggage of my heart, I would not have seen my need for humility and a humbling posture to receive the magnitude of these blessings and more. This is why no one can doubt God's power to me. I've discovered God's banquet table. I've tasted the Lord and have seen that He is good.

Taste and see that the Lord is good.

— Psalm 34:8

32

Chapter Four
FROM DEALING TO HEALING

There are many plausible steps to healing, but the only "one size fits all" remedy is the Lord Jesus Christ. For some, healing is a two-step dance and they've got it. For others, like me, it's a struggle, an ongoing dance lesson.

I had belonged to a dance team from early in my life, and even on my college team I don't remember ever learning a new step that didn't make me feel (and maybe look) a little awkward initially. But because I really wanted to dance, I took the time to do what needed to be done in practice to eventually get it right. I wanted to dance freely and beautifully, unhindered by awkwardness. But I had to go through some grueling lessons and consistent practice, which is no different from healing and growing through life's challenges.

When I was fifteen, I overdosed on prescription medication. In the depths of my depression, there was nothing anyone could say to convince me that God is real and that He would one day use my pain for His glory.

To my eyes, at that time, those who claimed to love God were the worst of them all—the hypocritical, the judgmental, those who didn't abide by the principles they preached . . . The only example I had of a "devout Christian" was my stepfather, who ushered my mother and me into church on Sundays, then got high on Mondays, pulling me with him into that confusing double lane, sharing drugs and a divine deity.

I was in eleventh grade when we lost our home due to my stepfather using all our money for his drugs and then leaving us. That's when the reality hit me of how we were living and why.

My mama and I shared a single twin mattress on my aunt's floor for months. I'd never seen anyone cry like my mama cried during that time. It broke my heart and awakened me to my mama's imperfections and also her breathtaking beauty. I crossed the milestone from naïve child to mindful young woman. That change felt rude, humbling, and also wonderfully awakening, all at the same time. A crazy thing for me, after seeing my mama's heart torn up, was seeing that she didn't carry a grudge, not for a day. She didn't spout, "all men are garbage," nor plant further seeds of distrust in my head about my stepfather or men in general. She didn't even complain one time! She just kept working and rebuilding herself by God's grace. She was by no means superwoman, but she was always super-empowered by His strength.

At sixteen, I had reached the point where I needed to discover for myself, as an individual *and for my wellbeing, who God is. It was at that intersection that my pain and destination collided. My deliverance did not occur at a pulpit but in a pit of darkness where I no longer wanted to reside.*

I cracked open the pages of the Bible and found the real Christ Jesus—who did not mirror the Christ that so-called "Christians" were painting. I discovered how Jesus authentically and unconditionally loved people from all walks of life, and how His love spread far and wide, from the castaways to those completely crippled by the chains of sin and the laws of religion. I saw that Jesus died for sinners, like me, without ever sinning Himself, and that He rose from the dead so I could rise from the ashes of my darkness and obscurities to LIFE as a new creature in Christ.

My mama doesn't consider herself a devout Christian. In fact, there are many things we disagree on regarding faith. However, I saw more of Christ in her than I've seen in some self-proclaimed ministers of the gospel.

My mama is selflessness epitomized, truly mirroring Jesus. Although she has only one biological child, she's a mother to many. She always taught me to fight for the underdog, as Christ did, and as the Bible directs us:

Speak up for those who cannot speak for themselves, for the rights of all who are destitute. Speak up and judge fairly; defend the rights of the poor and needy.

— Proverbs 31:8-9

When she struggles, she never complains. She's an example of the Proverbs 31 woman, and she doesn't need to wear a T-shirt that states this. Her life in action is the mirror reflection of Jesus through the explosion of His love that fills her soul and overflows to others.

Mama's selflessness is also what left her vulnerable in many situations, which made her an open target to those like my stepfather. She tried to stick it out for him, as her husband, because she believed it was the right thing to do. She had the insight to see that even his drug-addicted rages needed grace. But at that time, in my teens, I loathed her. Now, as an adult, I not only understand the position she was in but also respect it and her. She didn't know the magnitude of all that was happening with me behind the scenes in my teens—from my stepdad daily offering me drugs to becoming physically abusive against me.

Sometimes we've really got to go through the trenches to understand the thrust of God's placement, His grace, and His faithfulness. I'm sure if you asked my mama, she'd tell you she would go through every heartbreaking moment again to get to where she is now in her heart and mind. She's my *star*. She's not a woman of perfection, she's fallen multiple times, but she's a woman who *chooses* to get back up, no matter what daggers are thrown or what new dance steps challenge her. When I look at my mama now, in her most loving relationship with her husband, all I can do is smile with gratitude and peace. If I am but a glimmer of her reflection, I'm honored. Indeed, I am truly blessed!

All things do come together for our good and God's glory when we choose His ways.

Chapter Five
THE DANCE

I would like to walk you through some practical life dance steps I learned and practiced to mend the emotional wounds of my past. I hope you'll choose to dance with me.

As we go through these steps, take the time to truly extinguish the old ways that no longer fit you and utilize what you need to push through to true healing, wholeness, freedom, lasting love, peace, and God's unique purpose for *you*.

Even with zero experience and a track record of failure, the transformative power of Jesus Christ *will* give you a brand new, freeing dance. You simply need to take His hand, trust Him, allow Him to lead, and practice His 'grace-full,' steadfast steps.

> You turned my wailing into dancing; you removed
> my sackcloth and clothed me with joy.
> — PSALM 30:11

LOVE LETTERS

Prayer, praise, and worship . . .

> *Initially I had no idea how to pray. It felt*
> *unnatural, so I wrote letters to Jesus instead.*
> *Those were my prayers. The prayer letters began*
> *as interrogation toward Him, with a list of whys*
> *and asking how He could have allowed me to go*
> *through all I'd suffered. Those prayers in writing*
> *evolved into love letters, thanking Him for every*
> *good and bad experience.*
>
> *I'd pour my heart onto those pages with my*
> *tears. Tears that the Lord collected in a bottle*
> *(Psalm 56:8). Then I would read the letters*
> *aloud. There are many different kinds of dances*
> *and steps. I had simply chosen love letters to God*
> *as an intimate dance of prayer toward a deeper*
> *relationship with Him.*

I believe the Lord desires from each of us a daddy-daughter
dance in some form that is communicative with Him. His aim
is to meet us at the level we're currently functioning, just as a
loving, attentive daddy does for his daughter. Whether praying
silently, aloud, or writing love letters to Him, genuine heart-
poured prayer rarely sounds eloquent or profound, and that's
okay. His desire is simply for each of us to engage with Him in
an authentic flow of continuous conversation. There's no exact
formula other than simply being *real* with Him.

Even when you're in despair and at a loss for words in prayer,
you cannot allow the enemy of your mind (Satan) to silence
your prayers. You have an advocate who cries into God's ears on
your behalf. In such times, you'll find that He gently picks you

up and places your feet on top of His so you can continue the dance solely by the power of His strength and sure footing.

> The Spirit helps us in our weakness. We do not know what we ought to pray for, but the Spirit himself intercedes for us through wordless groans.
>
> — Romans 8:26

In companionship with prayer, your praise can resonate in many varying levels of volume and form. God interprets them all. I encourage you to dedicate a select time of your day to be intimate with God, not only by praying and studying the Bible for yourself but also praising and worshiping Him.

If you struggle with self-esteem, I encourage you to also pen love letters of godly truth to yourself. Deep wounding from abuse, and other atrocities of victimization, obliterates self-esteem and can cause you to believe the deceits of the perpetrator. The one who wounded you may have *manipulated your mind* into truly believing the abuse, the abandonment, or other assault to your spirit, was your fault. The evil one will whisper in your ear that you aren't going to be able to get back up, that you've done too many bad things, and that you're incapable of forgiving. These are all lies planted by the enemy of your soul. Remember, we do not fight against flesh and blood but against Satan, the prince of deceit and darkness and destruction (Ephesians 6:12).

The truth is: You *are* capable through Christ to overcome all your victimization:

> You, dear children, are from God and have overcome them, because the one who is in you is greater than the one who is in the world.
>
> — 1 John 4:4

You *are* able to "resist the devil, and he will flee from you" (James 4:7).

You were designed with a forgiving heart, "created to be like God in true righteousness and holiness" (Ephesians 4:24).

Exercise the power of God at work in you!

Writing love letters to yourself is a tool of power against the enemy. There's healing in speaking life and love to yourself. At first it may feel awkward, like those first dance lessons, but with practice your spirit will unravel the depths of your beauty in step with Christ.

Practice being kind to yourself, speaking words of benevolence that you wish others had spoken to you. Shower yourself with encouragement, compliments, and positive reinforcements that are truth in God's creation of you and transformation of your Spirit through Christ. **Until you learn to love yourself as Christ loves you, no one's love will ever be adequate.**

The truths that you say to yourself may not in the beginning sound like truth to you, but over time those truths you are daily planting in your mind will grow in your spirit. You will become one of God's "oaks of righteousness" that He promised in Isaiah 61. Believe that today is the first day of your *year of the Lord's favor* that will transform you to be gorgeous inside. This is for you:

The Year of the Lord's Favor

> The Spirit of the Sovereign Lord is on me, because the Lord has anointed me to proclaim good news to the poor. He has sent me to bind up the brokenhearted, to proclaim freedom for the captives and release from darkness

for the prisoners, to proclaim the year of the Lord's favor and the day of vengeance of our God, to comfort all who mourn, and provide for those who grieve in Zion—to bestow on them a crown of beauty instead of ashes, the oil of joy instead of mourning, and a garment of praise instead of a spirit of despair. **They will be called oaks of righteousness, a planting of the Lord for the display of his splendor.**

Isaiah 61:1-3 (author emphasis)

The Bible is filled with amazing truths about who God is for you, who *you* are in Him as a believer in Christ Jesus, and how He sees you as His beloved and GORGEOUS daughter. Below are a few of these biblical truths that you can read aloud to yourself in front of your mirror as affirmations of who you are in Christ in TRUTH. Navigate through these truths and fully embrace who you are in Him—gorgeous inside!

🌿 I am gorgeous in spirit and life. More than a mirror could ever reflect.

Your beauty should not come from outward adornment, such as elaborate hairstyles and the wearing of gold jewelry or fine clothes. Rather, it should be that of your inner self, the unfading beauty of a gentle and quiet spirit, which is of great worth in God's sight. (1 Peter 3:3-4)

🌿 I will carry myself with class.

I want women to adorn themselves with proper clothing, modestly and discreetly, not with braided hair and gold or pearls or costly garments, but rather by means of good works, as is proper for women making a claim to godliness. (1 Timothy 2:9-10)

🌿 My strength is from above.

My flesh and my heart may fail, but God is the strength of my heart and my portion forever. (Psalm 73:26)

🌿 I will not live in my yesterdays.

If anyone is in Christ, the new creation has come: The old has gone, the new is here! (2 Corinthians 5:17)

🌿 I will be a giver.

She opens her hand to the poor and reaches out her hands to the needy. She is not afraid of snow for her household, for all her household are clothed in scarlet. (Proverbs 31:20-21)

🌿 I am reborn.

Because of his great love for us, God, who is rich in mercy, made us alive with Christ even when we were dead in transgressions—it is by grace you have been saved. (Ephesians 2:4-5)

🌿 I may share in His sufferings, but I will also share in His glory.

If we are children, then we are heirs—heirs of God and co-heirs with Christ, if indeed we share in his sufferings in order that we may also share in his glory. (Romans 8:17)

🌿 I will bear much fruit.

I am the vine; you are the branches. If you remain in me and I in you, you will bear much fruit; apart from me you can do nothing. (John 15:5)

🌿 I will be confident. I will carry power, love, and self-discipline wherever I go.

The Spirit God gave us does not make us timid, but gives us power, love and self-discipline. (2 Timothy 1:7)

🌿 I can do ALL things through Christ. Not just some.

Be strong and courageous. Do not be afraid or terrified because of them, for the LORD your God goes with you; he will never leave you nor forsake you. (Deuteronomy 31:6)

I can do all this through him who gives me strength. (Philippians 4:13)

Looking at them Jesus said to them, "With people this is impossible, but with God all things are possible." (Matthew 19:26)

🌿 I am redeemed and forgiven by the grace of Christ.

In him we have redemption through his blood, the forgiveness of sins, in accordance with the riches of God's grace. (Ephesians 1:7)

🌿 I am in control of my words and will use them to help, not hinder.

She opens her mouth with wisdom, and the teaching of kindness is on her tongue. (Proverbs 31:26)

🌿 I will not concern myself with gossip. I will build up my sisters.

Women are to be worthy of respect, not malicious talkers but temperate and trustworthy in everything. (1 Timothy 3:11)

🌿 I am royalty.

In him we were also chosen, having been predestined according to the plan of him who works out everything in conformity with the purpose of his will. (Ephesians 1:11)

🌿 I am God's masterpiece, created for a larger purpose than myself.

We are God's handiwork, created in Christ Jesus to do good works, which God prepared in advance for us to do. (Ephesians 2:10)

🌿 God is my Provider; He supplies all my needs.

My God will supply all your needs according to His riches in glory in Christ Jesus. Now to our God and Father be the glory forever and ever. (Philippians 4:19-20)

🌿 I have nothing to worry about and everything to pray about.

Be anxious for nothing, but in everything by prayer and supplication with thanksgiving let your requests be made known to God. And the peace of God, which surpasses all comprehension, will guard your hearts and your minds in Christ Jesus. (Philippians 4:6-7)

✑

FORGIVENESS

Let's face it, you will not receive every "I'm sorry" you wish to hear. You will not be granted an apology from everyone who has ever forsaken you or trampled on your heart. Even still, you must make the choice to not allow hurt to steal your joy for one more second! Forgiveness is a gift you give to yourself. The misconception is that forgiveness is to free the conscience of the wrongdoer, when actually it frees the chains and shackles that restrain the victim from living a full life. Unbind your heart by releasing the bitterness and resentment that bind you from reaching the upper tiers of absolute happiness and harmony.

Perhaps you're thinking to yourself: *That's easy for you to say. You don't know what they did to me.* You're absolutely right; I have not walked a day in your shoes. Your individual experiences are your own and no one can claim to know exactly what you've endured, nor what you're feeling as a result of living in the trenches of your pain. However, what I can be certain about is the freedom and deliverance you'll encounter when you let go and let God handle the ache that has crippled you, and those who inflicted pain against you. Once the heaviness of your burdens is lifted, there's a lightness of spirit you never could have imagined. Allow God to lighten your burdens, beginning right now. Do you really want to carry that weight for the rest of your life?

> Forgiveness is a gift you give to yourself.

BURN IT UP

Write a letter to those who have hurt you and tell them you've chosen to no longer hold on to resentment, and share that you've forgiven them. Those letters aren't going anywhere beyond the grasp of your fingers and heaven, where the Lord will be rejoicing over the bondage you've chosen to break. Allow the letter-writing to be an act of laying all your wounds and forgiveness on the altar of God. When you've finished writing, burn them up (or shred them) as a sacrifice of love and trust in the One who made the greatest sacrifice for your freedom of heart and mind.

Now that you've forgiven and have released all the pain, it's done! It's now time to move forward and not look back.

DISCONNECT TO RECONNECT

While forgiveness is an essential step toward healing, the lacerations of your past, embedded within the folds and creases of your life, do not simply evaporate. A corporate career will not conceal your scars. An eventful, lively social life will not result in the erasure of your history of hurt. The areas of your life that you built as distractions from your unhappiness must be faced, and must be handed to the Lord.

Sometimes you've got to disconnect from the world to reconnect with your spirit and the One who calms the sea with His gentle, quiet voice. You must block out the interferences of your outside world in order to hone in on the internal—the depths of your heart—with God.

> Sometimes you've got to disconnect from the world to reconnect with your spirit and the One who calms the sea with His gentle, quiet voice.

Many pray faithfully for the answers to life's problems, but they won't stand still and silent long enough to hear God's responses. In addition to your prayer life you must intentionally form a meditative space, fit for you to *receive* messages of magnitude from Him. Relationship is a two-way conversation. The Lord does not aim to compete with the trifles of your job, social life, entertainment, and romantic interests. Log out of social media for a bit, cancel any superfluous plans that pull your attention from your healing, and get naked in vulnerability before the Lord. Reconnect with Him. He earnestly longs for your undivided attention and longs to love on you.

You will know you are healed when silence from the outside world feels like *peace*. When silence sounds like the screams of negativity in your mind, stand still and cry out to God even louder. Combat the disturbances of negativity with total yearning for His message for you and the biblical affirmations listed on the previous pages. Don't allow the plethora of messages from social media, magazines, satellite T.V., friends, and even family to compete with your divine Father-daughter dance. Exercise your right to disconnect from the world when led, and without feelings of guilt. Even Jesus took time-outs to rest alone with the Father. Responsibilities and social opportunities will still exist when you return, but so will the priceless gem of *peace*. Rest and dance in solitude with your Maker, who has the ability to ignite the fiery burn of harmony within your spirit.

THE BALANCE BATTLE

When I was single, I had so much more time to reserve for God. But when I got married and additional family commitments were added to my mix, my plate was very full. With more blessings came more responsibilities tugging to dwindle my time with God. I struggled with balance in my first year of marriage. It was an inner fight to reestablish my priorities and get to a place of peace in my spirit. It was an inner fight to ensure I replaced the emotional expenditures with divine deposits gained from time with God.

*Still, there were days I felt like I wasn't doing
enough—the house wasn't clean enough; I wasn't
pushing myself enough; I wasn't writing enough,
loving enough, giving enough . . . . When I have
those moments, I must remember that I have a
heavenly Father who says I'm more than enough
just as I am. And I remember that He said
I'm "fearfully and wonderfully made" (Psalm
139:14), and at the end of the day I am still His
daughter.*

Daily, give yourself the grace to understand that you'll never be perfect—but always loved.

Daily, give yourself the grace to understand that you'll never have it as together as your professional photo appears, but God sees you as gorgeous. While you're internally being perfected, remind yourself that He gives abundant grace with unfailing love through each new challenge and season of your life.

Daily, get the divine deposits that come from time spent with your Father. Divine deposits will enable you to best serve in the roles graciously gifted to you. Creating space for God in the center of your busyness brings balance. It's a fight to maintain balance between your needs and the needs of others, but balance is pivotal.

On one side of the scale we can give too much of ourselves. Without refueling, we become depleted, which creates a gap for bitterness. On the other side we can give too little of ourselves and become like a cork, blocking the flow of God through us. Balance is a key that will open healthy, grounded opportunities and imbalance will be a chain that binds.

REMEMBER TO REPEAT

> In this world you will have trouble. But take heart! I
> have overcome the world.
>
> — JOHN 16:33

No one is exempt from the struggles of life. Not every day will be gravy, nor easy to digest. Being genuinely happy is not equivalent to having no trials or tribulations. In fact, those who exhibit *true* joy and peace have probably endured the most. They remember to repeat daily (hourly, if needed) their *purposed decisions:*

- I will deposit the past in a lockbox that I empty daily into God's hands.

- I will overcome by letting go of my agony and giving it to God.

- I will give myself a break—grace—as God gives me.

- I will invest in my inner beauty by taking care of my spirit in Christ.

- I will take care of my spirit through prayer, worship, and daily feeding on the fruit of God's Spirit: "love, joy, peace, patience, kindness, goodness, faithfulness, gentleness, self-control" (Galatians 5:22-23 NASB).

Remember to repeat the redirecting of your focus by transferring your attention away from your pain and onto God. When you are feeding on His Word, He is giving Himself to you. In worship and prayer you are giving yourself to Him. His Son, Jesus, gives eternal hope and daily encouragement—His live-producing nutrients. Don't try to survive off of yesterday's bread. His Holy Spirit gives direction, so don't allow a day to pass without generating conversation with the Lord.

> The mirror will always be too fickle to reflect your true beauty.

Remember to repeat putting off fear and putting on courage. God has promised that He will never leave nor forsake you (Hebrews 13:5). When it seems like your boat is lost at sea, deserted in the eye of the storm, remember to repeat to yourself that God is right there, waiting on your call to Him (Mark 4:38). When you feel your life taking a nosedive, like an aircraft headed for destruction, remember to repeat to yourself that God is waiting in the cockpit to take over the controls of your life.

If you need visual affirmations, write biblical reminders on post-it notes. Stick one on your mirror to remind you that the mirror will always be too fickle to reflect your true beauty—the beauty God created in you.

WHAT GOES IN

Exposure is crucial to the way our spirits develop and how they heal. Remember to repeat the guarding of your heart! Have you ever noticed that when you watch junk on TV or listen to derogatory music, your spirit feels heavy afterward? For a while, your head was bobbing to the beat as you smiled and hummed along. Before you realized it, you were beginning to talk and act in ways that reflected what you ingested. We often fail to realize that while derogatory beats can be bangin' and cynical clips can be comical, we're subconsciously planting bombs that will eventually explode.

No one wakes up with intentions to be misogynistic, promiscuous, deceitful, or immoral. But the truth is, constantly repeated messages of negativity and ungodliness *are* released into our lives, our minds, and our hearts every day through many different avenues we utilize. Dark attitudes and messages latch onto us and fill us, and we unknowingly reflect that darkness. This tactic of the enemy keeps us in a place of perpetual pain, despair, hopelessness, and numbness—dead spirits in the valley of dry bones (Ezekiel 37:1-14). Are we putting as much effort into knowing and living the powerful Word of God?

You may honestly feel "it's *just* music" or "it's *just* a movie." You may ask, *what's the big deal?* The big deal is that you have a *divine purpose* to fulfill. But when you consume these channels, you open the door for negativity to feed into your life that will work to destroy that divine purpose. **The food of the enemy fuels his power *over* you, but the food of Lord fuels His power *in* you to overcome the enemy and fulfill your divine destiny.** His living Word will ignite healing light and fulfilling power into your spirit that will burn powerfully into your circumstances and relationships. His power at work in you *will* defeat the evil one.

In the end, there will be only one winner: God. Will you be on His side?

The same principle of ingestion applies to your body. 1 Corinthians 6:19-20 says, "Do you not know that your body is a temple of the Holy Spirit, who is in you, whom you have received from God? You are not your own; you were bought at a price. Therefore, honor God with your bodies."

Your temple needs to be preserved and protected, just as your spirit. You cannot afford to be afflicted with preventable illnesses and diseases due to poor eating habits, drug use, and drinking habits, or have soul ties with the soulless through your body by way of sex outside of marriage. Purity in every way is part of your purpose.

SEEK COUNSEL

You were not meant to live life alone. You do not have to remain introverted and alone with seeping scars. Seek counsel from those wisely fit to speak into the wounded areas of your life. Seek and take full advantage of godly counselors, mentors, coaches, support groups, and other ministries such as books and hotlines. However, in an effort to maintain a healthy balance, do not *rely* on others to determine the amount of healing or treatment you'll require to recover or change. What I've discovered in my life is that some areas need just a day to transform while other areas need ongoing prayer, repetitive action, patience, and at times other people to assist.

Each and every individual becomes scarred and each heals differently. Trust God to always be the antidote and do not be afraid or ashamed to admit you need guidance. Be proactive to seek help from others when you need it.

> The way of fools seems right to them, but the wise listen to advice.
>
> — PROVERBS 12:15

Chapter Six

GIFTWRAPPED
FOR GOD

Let's say you've taken the steps presented in the previous chapters, you're practicing them, and you've reached a point of healing where you're now better equipped to direct others toward a destination of healing. Because you're *gorgeous inside*, you have the eyes of compassion and understanding. A woman's innate nature is to nurture, and that nurturing spirit is an astounding thing. Think about the type of intrinsic character one must possess to withstand the trials of victimization and yet still love wholeheartedly. *True love* has no fear factor great enough to stop you from making that leap to loving others, for "there is no fear in love" (1 John 4:18). At times, your compassion is so great that you not only attempt to plant seeds in others but also continuously water them, and even wait around for them to harvest. Caution: In our persistence to heal others by being *too* present in their pain, we can inadvertently lose the balance we've worked to achieve, and become an enabler to them.

We are enablers when we do not allow the hurting to do their part and fully allow God to do His. Who are we to step in the way of His work? Are you strong enough, courageous enough, trusting in God enough to let go of someone when you realize your strength alone is not enough?

It's perfectly natural to want to help those close to you, even when their toxic choices are hurting you. Often we feel we can save our tormented loved ones. We truly believe we can carry the afflicted to the finish line. We want them to get better, as we have, but our well-meaning help can actually transform into "enabling" because, realistically, we cannot stand to see our loved ones hit rock bottom. We don't want to see them suffer, perhaps because we know so well ourselves what rock bottom looks and feels like. **What we must remember is that what we deem as "reaching out a helping hand" can be interpreted by the afflicted as permitting them to continue their downward spiral.** We don't realize that we're sometimes holding on to our loved one's potential first, rather than their healing. We choose what's easier for them (and us) rather than what's *best* for both. How much of your own healing work came through your own intentional actions?

The very changes we've achieved in ourselves that we want to see transpire in another person, whether hoping they attain a closer relationship with Christ or get rid of a toxic habit, will often not occur because we're *too* present and hands-on in their garden for them to take ownership and responsibility to tend it themselves. In many cases, troubled ones must crawl through their own miry clay—as you likely had to do—to come out clean and reshaped on the other side. There's only one lump of unshaped and messy clay on the Potter's wheel at any given time—either yourself or the one you wish to change. The fact is, you cannot change another person. That's God's job.

Being too present in someone else's garden, road-blocking their recovery and growth by offering them options, is actually selfish of you and dangerous for them. Do you remember these truths from your own journey to healing? When we repeatedly offer to be a loved one's Plan B, we're often the very reason they're not choosing Plan A. To be honest, people *right next to you* are possibly not changing because you're offering them a Plan B option. Do you, and do *they*, really have that time to waste?

DEDICATED DECISIONS

Just as there are some flowers that grow through concrete, there are others who grow only seasonally. Before a drug addict embarks on treatment and recovery, she must make a dedicated decision *for herself* that *she wants* freedom for herself—apart from the influences of all others in her life. Regardless of family members' begging, tears, and prayers, and the judgments of colleagues and friends, the wounded, the afflicted, and the addicted will not let go of their monsters until they personally, individually desire to take that step toward their freedom and make a determined decision to do so. If you have come that far in your *own* healing, was your freedom due to your own personal decision and dedication to do the necessary work or did your freedom come through the efforts of someone else tending to your internal garden? Are you among those who are continually tending your own garden and continually growing fruit of the Spirit, or are you growing only seasonally?

> Therefore, my dear friends, as you have always obeyed . . . continue to work out your salvation with fear and trembling.
>
> — PHILIPPIANS 2:12

There will be times when you do not need to undertake certain challenges but fully trust that *God's got this*. Your destiny is not attached to guarding the garden inside someone else; the one garden you are eternally indebted to is the one inside *you*.

Because we don't always understand this, God must at times take us on a detour to teach us this fundamental lesson: Learn to discern when it's time to say to someone you care about, "No more!"

The magnificent thing about the Lord is that He doesn't need your help to be God. Sometimes He actually wants you to put your face in a corner and listen to His command *to stay in your own lane.* "Be still, and know that I am God" (Psalm 46:10).

Do not strive to be a milepost on a single road; strive to be a fork, that people may turn one way or another when facing Christ in you. Ask the Lord to use you as a vessel for others to take positive rather than enabling action in their lives. Ask God to let you represent a crossroad. And when you cannot discern between lending a helping hand and removing your hands altogether, this simple yet sometimes complex five-word phrase is always best to follow: let go and let God.

> *Do not strive to be a milepost on a single road; strive to be a fork, that people may turn one way or another when facing Christ in you.*

Did you know that the biblical meaning of the number five is GRACE—a five-letter word meaning "favor?" Another five-letter, *Jesus*, is the One who ushered grace into our world, into your life. His grace can produce God's best in you—if you choose Him. His favor toward you includes choices, a crossroad, and a spirit of discernment and discipline, which is the same favor you can extent to yourself, and to the hurting, by allowing God to work in them as He works in you.

Stepping back from challenged loved ones, however, does *not* mean you must fully up and leave them—absolutely not! We need one another. Your loved one still needs your compassion, your reassurance, and encouragement to continually put their heart and faith in Christ, but your loved one's first "solo steps" of faith are critical to their healing and freedom. Your "no" can be the suffering person's very reason for saying "yes" to the Potter's wheel on which God will produce a gorgeous vessel to be filled with an enriched life.

> *I kept going back. It was as if the blatant proof of my man's infidelity wasn't enough to keep me away. I mean, I was no angel after all, but I knew I didn't deserve this. Feeling his presence and comfort became more important than my own well-being and self-worth. Even if the highs lasted for only mere minutes or seconds, I craved them. I was needy and also an enabler to my abuser.*

Lust and emotional neediness are drugs that keep you locked up in a dirty holding cell, trapped in a place of enabling your abuser. You may argue, "But you don't know how good he is *most* times, how he *truly* loves me, how he takes *care* of me, how he *helps* me take care of my kids, how much *fun* we have in between the bad times . . . . The bad times are not really so bad compared to all the good, so . . . ."

The temporary fulfillment that lust and neediness bring is such an emotional and physical rush that it never occurs to you during that high that it's truthfully only a camouflage of the real thing. True fulfillment is birthed from pure love, which is the clean, just, balanced, powerful love of God. Lust and neediness disguise themselves as genuine love until it's time to make a sacrifice. There's a clear parting of the sea between lust and authentic love when the going gets tough. For example: When the party ends you either choose to bail out, because the fun is over, or you choose to face the fact that your house is now a wreck and someone needs to take responsibility to clean it up and restore it to its original beauty and purity. Your spirit, your being *is your house*. How do you truly want to live in it?

> *Years passed before it dawned on me that I was trying to fill a void with shallow declarations of love that were really just well-cloaked episodes of lust and neediness. The void inside me was impossible to fill because it was an emptiness that could only be filled by God. Only He could convert my scars into stars.*

You are not required to be an airport in the lives of others, forced to work around their delays, arrivals, departures, and demands. If someone gives you the ultimatum "ride or die," ask yourself why you would ever want to invest your time, energy, or heart into such a person. Someone who is in the business of making emotional, physical, and/or sexual demands on your life may try to convince you that you should feel fortunate to be in their life and that you're receiving the ultimate prize, or that you should simply "take what you can get." These are examples of manipulation. Your abuser's worst nightmare is the day you come to the realization that you are "fearfully and wonderfully made" (Psalm 139:14) and that you are empowered by the Holy Spirit within you to be courageous to take the steps to live and thrive in God's BEST for you. Once you realize your worth as God's creation, and your worth as His adopted daughter—a divine princess!—when you have accepted Jesus Christ as your

> Choose how you will use your royal position in this life.

Savior, your royal position can *never* be stolen nor your portion depleted. But . . . you get to *choose how you will use* your royal position in this life. Will you choose God's best for you in every aspect, or allow the enemy to win?

> For those who are led by the Spirit of God are the children of God. The Spirit you received does not make you slaves, so that you live in fear again; rather, the Spirit you received brought about your adoption to sonship. And by him we cry, "Abba, Father." The Spirit himself testifies with our spirit that we are God's children. Now if we are children, then we are heirs—heirs of God and co-heirs with Christ, if indeed we share in his sufferings in order that we may also share in his glory.
>
> — ROMANS 8:14-17

We cripple people who are capable of walking because we choose to carry them.

— CHRISTIE WILLIAMS

Chapter Seven
NO NEW FRIENDS?

Although we should tread lightly around potential negativity in day-to-day life, and perfect the art of discerning situations to ensure we're not enabling, or staying stuck and stagnating, we must also be sure we aren't so guarded that we become closed off. God has placed in your life specific people to encourage you, pray for you, and hold you accountable—and for you to do the same for them. But society has conditioned women to act with paranoia and become hypersensitive to the possibility that there's always someone who's "after" them. We've created a mass of women who feel they cannot open up to anyone. They safeguard themselves to the extent that they're incapable of showing genuine love in friendship to other women.

Think about how many times you've heard women described as "bitchy." You may have used that description yourself from time to time. How many times have you entered a room full of' women, both in social, professional, and spiritual settings, and instantly felt countless eyes "sizing you up," assessing your intentions, judging how you measure up and where you may have the upper hand?

Where did we go wrong as women of God that we can no longer trust each other? Was it the ex-best friend who spilled your secrets or took your man? Was it reality TV and their side commentaries that set the example and assured us that we can't trust others? Was it the noose of abuse?

Whatever the cause of our withdrawal from one another, we must get back to the truth that we need each other as God designed. We need to get back to the place of authentic godly love—"agape" love, the purest and highest form of God's love for humankind, our love for Him, and our love for each other.

Although the flesh says, "only support those who support you," is that attitude the true representation of Christ? If God had said, "only through works you will be healed," would you ever feel like your actions were good enough? Would you simply stop at one hug to a stranger?

We need each other, ladies, to get back to a place of principality, honor, reverence, accountability, and true agape love.

If you only embrace and support those who embrace and support you, who makes the first move? *Someone* needs to have the fortitude to step forward and change the climate of how women approach and treat each other. Where is your thermostat set for those who cross your path?

> *I used to push people away, and then I'd wonder why I was always lonely. I'd never open up. Then I'd complain about how no one understood me. I'd never make eye contact and yet I swore no one liked me. I was an uninviting person to those I encountered in my adult life. I bolted doors that could have led to greater openings and avenues. I was a misrepresentation of agape love and*

sisterhood. So how could I expect to attract these characteristics? I had to come to the realization that my insecurity was no excuse and that I alone had the power to set the climate around me.

Insecurity is not contagious; it's not passed on by others, even if their actions are unfavorable. Though the reason behind your insecurity may be justifiably heart-wrenching, that reason , is in the past. In the here and now, you must deal with and settle your insecurities in order to more completely heal and to take hold of the power God has placed in you to love yourself and others. Insecurity is a poisonous weed crafted and planted in you by Satan, the evil one. Only you can choose to cut it out at its root and burn it up. The fire of God's power in you is His glory: to burn off everything that hinders you from being all He created you to be, and to shine brightly—warmly welcoming— to draw others out of the cold darkness and into His healing and fulfilling. You have the power, by your free will, to light that fire. Will you?

I encourage you to ask yourself: What am I doing that's shutting people out, especially other women? How can I be a better sister? How can I learn to love myself more so I can love on others, even when it's difficult? Don't get this twisted: "Bad company corrupts good character" (1 Corinthians 15:33), but loving people as Christ loves them, at their current level, does not mean you have to *endorse* where they stand or how they behave. We've all behaved badly, which is exactly why Christ died for us—to make us new; so why do so many of us walk around with bulletproof vests when no one is even shooting? Let's break away from the cold, steel bolts and chains of distrust, and learn from Christ what it looks like to truly "love each other as I have loved you" (John 15.12).

> Speaking the truth in love, we will grow to become
> in every respect the mature body of him who is the
> head, that is, Christ.
>
> — EPHESIANS 4:15

A friend who constantly pats you on the back, even when you're wrong, is no friend at all. Harsh truth from a friend is better than applause from an enemy because it evokes necessary change. Jesus asks us to speak truth—in love—because at the core of all things created is God's love, for "God is love" (1 John 4:8). Seek sisters who don't simply check to see if your outfit is "fly." Seek those who are firelights and willing to hold you accountable for your character rather than for your clothes.

Death to the "girl power" mentality that is shouting through media to women and girls: all I need is *me*, *my* goals, and *my* girls. What about us fulfilling the roles God called us to as royal, divinely-appointed women young and aged? If we keep excluding people because of their credentials, or because they're not exactly like us, then what is the purpose of "family"—the "one body" of Christ that we're supposed to emulate as believers?

> Harsh truth from a friend is better than applause from an enemy because it evokes necessary change.

> In Christ we, though many, form one body, and each
> member belongs to all the others.
>
> — ROMANS 12:5

The truth is: an overindulged confidence screams with insecure undertones. The suggestion here is not for you to be a revolving door, moving in and out of extreme attitudes, beliefs, and behaviors, but rather work to stay centered in Christ.

The lyrics "No new friends" by hip hop artist DJ Khaled is, in my opinion, the most senseless tagline ever popularized. It promotes the disregard of sisterhood and camaraderie in favor of self-absorption and preoccupation.

Uncompromising *balance* is everything.

An overindulged confidence screams with insecure undertones.

Let's break away from the cold, steel bolts and chains of distrust, and learn from Christ what it looks like to truly "love each other as I have loved you" (JOHN 15.12).

Chapter Eight
STAYING IN YOUR OWN LANE

Let's get this clear: there is only one *you*. The sooner you discern and embrace this, the sooner you'll walk in complete and utter freedom. This world attempts to feed you garbage that influences you and misleads you down crooked paths. Everywhere you turn you're met with worldly standards that try to convince you to fill molds you do not fit into. You were created with unique motive and a divine purpose to fulfill before you were even formed in your mother's womb (Jeremiah 1:5). He deliberately set you apart for a reason, and only you can choose to fulfill or reject His purpose for your life. So if you're intent on trying to fit in, or forcing the individuality that already exists in you, I have to ask you why.

Have you ever noticed that the outcome is often unfulfilling when you attempt to mimic another person in any way, including the attempt to achieve something outside your unique gifting that brings success to another person? If you feel cheated when you see success in someone, it's because you want to fit into *their* mold, with their particular talents not meant for you. What is for *you* is for *you*. What is for someone else is theirs. You are not anointed to be the image of anyone else; you are anointed to be the one and only, unique *you*. You were fashioned in a precise image for a precision purpose. Imagine that! Envision the Lord molding a purpose just for *you*, and anointing *you* to fulfill it. Walk in that authority, but not with self-centered pride. The opposite of insecurity and jealousy is also the opposite of humility, which is pride. Walk with grace and dignity in humility that comes from knowing and valuing who you are in Christ—a servant with Him—and an attitude of gratitude.

For example, my purpose (condensed) is writing, teaching, and encouraging others. Many times, without thought, quotes and quips come to me, planted by the Holy Spirit. My writing style lacks tradition; it's forthright. What some people may spell out in paragraphs pours through me in a sentence. Here's my point by example: I admire many authors and contemporary artists who are truly making a difference, but I find that when I try to write like them, or say or do something as they would, it doesn't have nearly the same effect as when it comes from the original source: God, speaking in and through me . To be effective, I must stay in my lane, the one He put me in to fulfill His unique purpose for me.

I'm not graced to speak on finances, so I don't delve into that area. I'm newly married, so I won't touch on what it takes to maintain lifelong matrimony. These pipes of mine sing best in the shower and unashamedly during praise and worship, but trust me when I assure you that you will never catch me trying to record the next hit, even with Auto-Tune. You see, I'm striving to master the skill of staying in my lane.

Although "stay in your own lane" may sound restrictive, it can actually propel you to become limitless. If you've taken the time to explore and discover your unique God-given gifts, you can more wisely utilize your time to refine those gifts.

Stop comparing yourself to others. When the door of comparison opens insecurity and jealousy enters. Social media has readily put infinite information at our fingertips that waters these poisonous seeds. We can have window-seat views into the lives of others almost instantaneously through advancing technology. Each of us occasionally looks online to see how others are living, what they're doing and accomplishing, even out of mere curiosity. While we need others in order to learn and grow, "as iron sharpens iron" (Proverbs 27:17), and while others can influence and motivate us positively, their path and pace should not be the basis by which we define our own. Stop comparing your life to the window-view aspects that others share publically about their lives. No one is perfect, but each of us was born with God-given gifts and a divine purpose.

> When the door of comparison opens insecurity and jealousy enters.

Even the most successful person in their lane began with a crawl. Remember this: **Agility trumps ability**. Do not tap out when life gets hard. Pass the test and keep going in the direction God has called you to go.

> He makes me as surefooted as a deer, enabling me to stand on mountain heights.
>
> — PSALM 18:33

The concept of staying in your own lane is not to suggest you should quit trying new things or avoid being teachable. Just because you may not perform with exceptional ability in a certain area does not mean you should never practice or develop that area of interest. However, in the aim to be extraordinary in the capacity God has created and called you, treading your track *does* mean that you must refine and cultivate your divine purpose *before* you choose to hop from one project to the next, from one zone to another.

No one has an assortment of experiences, nor a vision, purpose, or anointing, exactly like yours. Walk in that authority. **One can't clone what they weren't meant to own.** *So what* if they hate on you?! People often mock what they can't jock. Never focus your eyes so intently on another's lane that you cannot see what is right in front of you on your own path. The very thing we're often ungrateful for is the same thing another is praying for. Stay mindful, grateful, and humble through all seasons.

Regardless of your lane, it neither increases nor decreases your worth or importance in comparison with anyone else. Be who God created *you* to be

> Be who God created **you** to be uniquely

uniquely and never look down on your portion or someone else's. A woman with this top-tier level of self-awareness can *genuinely* encourage her sisters, respect her brothers, and bring favor to her husband. She does not concern herself with tearing others down or wasting her time with senseless gossiping. She does not compromise her character by smearing the names of others. She has experienced being on the receiving end of such insults and attacks. **Her strength is her humility and she feels no need to flex any other muscles.**

> The very thing we're often ungrateful for is the same thing another is praying for.

Your lane will provide you with the wisdom necessary to love everyone while successfully accomplishing what God designed specifically for you. If you're unsure about the nature of your lane—what is God's plan for me?—I urge you to ask Him and be proactive in getting the answer by stepping out in faith and trying new experiences to discover your gifts. He will confirm those when you're actively seeking Him in prayer and action.

> What good is it . . . if someone claims to have faith but has no deeds? Can such faith save them? Suppose a brother or a sister is without clothes and daily food. If one of you says to them, "Go in peace; keep warm and well fed," but does nothing about their physical needs, what good is it? In the same way, faith by itself, if it is not accompanied by action, is dead.
>
> — James 2:14-17

> I love those who love me, and those who seek me find me.
>
> — Proverbs 8:17

Have you noticed that the moment you step out in faith is the moment that attacks hit you left and right? Sometimes we feel like we can't get a break! If it's not one thing it's another. Attacks are not by chance. The enemy will literally use your greatest weaknesses and temptations to unleash some of the most challenging complications in your life. But once you have identified his tactics, his manipulations are no match for your faith, "The one who is in you is greater than the one who is in the world" (I John 4:4). And his tactics are no match for your prayers. Prayer is the 'pow'erful punch against the enemy.

> The prayer of a righteous person is powerful and effective.
>
> — James 5:16

71

Oftentimes what you're doing in your lane has no respect to time. It's as if time freezes and your spirit is in complete tranquility while you're engulfed in your gift. Conversely, it may also be marked with the greatest obstacles. But working together as "one body" with Christ Jesus (Ephesians 2:6), we have encouragement and support. Like the human body, the body of Christ has many unique parts, each that must be healthy and active to do what it was intended in harmony with the whole body. The purpose we *all* share in common is the duty to edify and build up the kingdom of God. Your unique part is essential, so stay in your lane.

Chapter Nine

ON THE VERGE
OF YOUR MERGE

When on the verge of your merge—the progression of your walk—it's pivotal that you carefully watch what you internalize. You can no longer listen and talk to just anyone about your life's concerns. Some people are not equipped to speak into every area of your life. Do not allow loyalty and habit to pressure you into staying stagnant with last season's word. The reality is that some people are not destined to go where you're going. These same people may attempt to join forces on your back, and if you do not draw clear boundaries you may end up hauling their junk into your lane, damaging your process and growth as well as theirs.

Once you've established *your* lane and comparison has left the building, and you're working in harmony with the other members of the body of Christ, you can wave hello to a new arena of opportunity. "A gift opens the way and ushers the giver into the presence of the great" (Proverbs 18:16). How does this verse relate to you and your lane? When you pursue Christ with your whole heart, and embark on a journey in your lane, provision will follow you. Provision comes in many forms that reach well beyond money.

You do not have to chase things and people. What you chase runs. Instead, be so committed to the process and purpose of your lane that opportunities track *you*. Be fastened toward your mark. However, ensure that attaining your goals does not become your idol. Ask God for continual focus and redirection so your attention is not lured toward something that will cause you to lose sight of His will over your life. "Press on toward the goal to win the prize for which God has called [*you*] heavenward in Christ Jesus" (Philippians 3:14, author insert).

Chapter Ten

BECOMING YOUR OWN STEPPING STONE

First, don't confuse your "own stepping stone" with your "own lane." These are two different points. Your own stepping stone is you learning to step more independently from your neediness and dependency on those close to you (and their dependency on you). To have people who will pray for you and encourage you is important and uplifting, but you must advance to a point where you master self-encouragement. Learn how to be your own cheerleader when no one is watching and you're feeling like you're trapped in a losing spree. Get this ingrained in your mind: The team of God and you is a full stadium.

While God encourages us to seek wise counsel and be teachable, you must not become trapped or stagnated by waiting on confirmations from others. Who are they to approve which direction you should or should not go, rather than simply guiding and teaching? God alone has ordained in you His purpose. In pursuing His purpose you'll need encouragement, wise counsel, and teaching; but beware: There will be times when others will attempt to lead you when you have *no clear indication* in your spirit whether their direction is leading you to follow the Shepherd or the wolf in sheep's clothing.

God is the only One who is *always* reliable and true; the purpose of His Spirit in you is to teach, lead, and intercede (John 14:26, Matthew 4:1, Romans 8:26). People are capricious, but God's plans for your life are clear and unchanging. **If God said it, why are you trying to bed it? Never put God's word—His direction within your spirit—to rest**. When people are trying to get the best of you, and your self-defeating thoughts are trying to get what's left of you, this is the time to hold more firmly to God's unchanging hand and hear His unchanging voice.

I know it hurts when your MVP goes missing or begins to look like opposition, but this, again, is a redirection toward Christ that reminds you that you are nothing without Him (John 15:5) but can do "all things" through Him (Philippians 4:13). Your light cannot be turned on or off by the applause of anyone. Do not take the fight in strife. Learn to call on the Lamp within you and rest in His promises.

> In all your ways submit to him, and he will make
> your paths straight.
> —PROVERBS 3:6

Our human nature seeks love and appreciation. There is no foul in desiring the companionship or adoration of loved ones. However, when your self-value is contingent on the validation of another, this can lead to a place of desperation. Besides, no one's sweet-talking their way into heaven. At some point, in order to advance in various areas of your life, you must cultivate self-love—the love Christ has extended to you—and exercise reliance on loving yourself as He loves you. A word of encouragement after a failure is worth far more than an hour of praise after a triumph, and that word of encouragement doesn't always have to come from someone else. Seek positive reinforcements from the cheerleader already residing in you.

> *Writing a book was one of the loneliest processes that God has ever entrusted to me and given me the grace to experience. Days and days of blank pages could pass by with no one to shovel out constructive and encouraging reminders to keep going. But inside me the madness ensued.*

The often lonely process of producing your purpose can be likened to an overdeveloped baby in your womb, well past the due date, with no modern medicine or engineered tools to birth it for you. This is exactly how I felt at times while baking the bun (this book) and birthing it. Often it was entirely up to me to encourage myself, and likewise it's entirely up to you to encourage yourself. It's up to you to discover or create a quiet space in this loud, industrial, technological world to be able to listen to and *hear* the substance and voice of God's Spirit in you, and the voice of your own spirit in communication with His.

In the Bible, a woman who suffered from incessant bleeding listened to the voice inside her. She had been written off by her community. She had continued to bleed for so many years that people just assumed her condition was terminal and her days were numbered. There was seemingly no hope for this woman, but she mustered the faith to encourage herself. She spoke life and truth to herself that Jesus was her answer. She could have retreated, accepted the beliefs of others, accepted that she was never going to live a normal life, that she wasn't going to be blessed, and that her healing was too farfetched. After all, she had endured this condition for so long. But, discounting public opinion, she pushed through the crowd to find Jesus and courageously, with faith, reached out and touched His garment.

Instantly, she was healed.

Amazingly, in her darkness and loneliness, she did not give up. She thrust her way through the patronizing crowd toward the Light. It was by her choosing—her faith in action—that she was healed!

It can be difficult to embrace the darkness when it's pitch black and all you can feel is your heart racing. Sometimes when you're stumbling through the wilderness, there truly seems to be no way out and you seriously consider aborting the mission. The mission has collected so many tears, tried to constrain you with countless shackles, and taken a few people you thought would be there forever. Still, there's this voice inside you that won't allow you to give up. Hearing that voice can be difficult when you're struggling in the maze of adversity, but it's calling out to you, even through your pain.

You must never forget that although some pain is self-inflicted, there are other struggles that are divinely orchestrated to glorify God—like the bleeding woman's. Not just anyone can handle what you've endured. **Some paths were specifically assigned to your life because you were the chosen vessel to carry that testimony**. And guess what? Learning to inspire yourself is pivotal! Even in simple tasks or ventures you've considered, you don't need to wait on others to make a move with you. *Become your own stepping stone.* Waiting on another individual can keep you bleeding for years, sitting at the station watching opportunities pass you by on the tracks of life. Don't wait on a casual cosigner to sign you off with their stamp of approval. *Move when God tells you to move.* When you step out in faith, you're never alone. He is always with you.

Chapter Eleven
BIRTHING A BLESSING

During the development of our dreams there are changes and advances that take place—like a mother's pregnancy—toward birthing those dreams.

A mother's body undergoes three stages during pregnancy. Metaphorically, so do fulfilling your dreams. Will you be fully prepared to push your vision into reality and parent that vision when the time comes? No matter how rough a past pregnancy may have been, or how much it may have hurt to push, all will be worth it once that beautiful baby is in the mother's arms.

The first trimester of pregnancy is crucial: the stage in which the body is experiencing many changes hormonally, physically, and mentally. Whether pregnancy was planned or not, the "yes" on the test can be a lot to digest. Unfortunately, the first trimester is when new mothers are most susceptible to miscarriage, so on the advice of health professionals, most women choose wisely who they will share the news with in those early weeks. The same philosophy should be applied in regard to carrying a newly-conceived dream. When God plants a vision in you, sometimes it's so farfetched it's hard for even you to believe, so not just anyone should know just yet. He will prune from your life the factors and people not meant to be present in this early stage, and it's your responsibility to protect your 'baby,' and care for yourself throughout the vision-growing process. A mother will follow her obstetrician's advice on nutrition, rest, and exercise to help ensure a viable pregnancy and healthy baby—as well as a healthy mama to care for that baby. Not just anything should enter a mother's mouth.

The same principles should be applied to nurturing your vision and yourself to ensure the vision's viability.

> *When I was sixteen years old, God told me that I would be an author for His glory. At that time, I couldn't see how that was going to happen. I was a hot mess-and-a-half. I didn't write with the skill level of renowned authors I read. I didn't live a life worth reading about. My mind was flooded with doubt. If I had disclosed the undertaking of this book to someone back then, I most likely would have terminated the mission.*

Your dream must not be aborted. If the enemy cannot abort God's plans in your life, he will attempt to derail them by accelerating them. But God's timing is always perfect. This doesn't mean *you* will be perfect. He does not utilize the perfect for His calling; He attempts to perfect the called by using their imperfections as inspirations.

Once your vision has been birthed and you're parenting it, everything you do your vision will emulate. So what can you do during the 'pregnancy' process of your vision to become a better follower of Christ, and eventually a solid leader? You will need to follow God's instructions on spiritual nutrition, rest, and exercise to grow and birth a healthy, viable dream. No longer can you afford to do some of the things you used to do, for there's new life at stake. As the surrogate parent of your vision, you're a leader in the responsibility of handling your God-given blessing with the utmost care. Not just anything should be permitted to enter your mind and heart. He will ask you to sit still in His presence to better learn to distinguish His voice from all others and to patiently feed your spirit the nutrients it needs. Everything you consume, your dream consumes. Redirect negative thoughts or transform them into positives. You control your emotions; they don't control you. Are you taking care of your 'baby?' Are you taking care of yourself?

A mother's obstetrician doesn't give her all the guidance and information she'll need for the entire pregnancy and birth on the first visit. Likewise, when God conceives a purpose in you, all the confidence and steps you'll need to fulfill His mission are not usually handed to you all at once. The details are developed through time and wisdom, and it's your duty to not only guard that baby but also wait on God's delivery date. Working outside of His timing can decapitate a vision. Your dream is still in the beginning stages of vital organ production. The umbilical cord is not ready to be cut until He brings the vision to full term. You must step back and exercise patience in the development period and trust Him in the growth process. Just as a mother trusts the specialist to position the ultrasound perfectly on her belly to hear the life beat of her baby's heart, you must trust God to be the very LIFE of your dream. Have conviction that The Specialist—the Doctor of your destiny—is equipped to handle what He has ordained in you, and that He will be faithful to equip you to parent the vision.

In the second trimester of pregnancy, the risk of miscarriage decreases tremendously. Friends and family members have been notified of the news and the parents have begun to make environmental adjustments to accommodate their new, precious life that will be arriving in a few months. They're able to hear their baby's heartbeat, discover the gender, and the mother feels movement inside her. It's not uncommon in these weeks for her to visit her doctor or midwife often. She begins to gain a substantial amount of weight, her changing hormones have her trapped on an emotional roller coaster, and suddenly she realizes her life will never be the same.

In the third trimester of pregnancy, carrying a baby begins to become downright uncomfortable for a mother. Her enlarged belly makes restful sleep practically impossible. Her back hurts, her ankles are swollen, her breasts are huge, and she's always hungry! She begins to think to herself, *dang, when's this baby coming out?!*

While growing your purpose, get comfortable with being uncomfortable. No matter how many obstacles try to knock you off course, no matter who does not approve of your dream, remember that your 'baby' is ALIVE! Patience is the mother's virtue. Do not despise your vision process; appreciate that in every step of the journey there's growth, stretching, and preparation. Every stage, every change, every tear, and every time you have to get back up and encourage yourself will be worth your perseverance and pain.

We can have a birth plan for exactly how we want our purpose to be delivered, but oftentimes those plans proceed differently than we'd hoped or imagined. God's plan of order, however, always exceeds our understanding. A mother may have wanted a natural birth but life's complications may have turned her plans into a needed C-section in order to deliver a healthy baby, and mother. As much as you try to anticipate what's coming in birthing your vision, you don't have the sight or mind of your

Creator. You've got to submit your will to Christ in every aspect of the purpose-birthing process.

"I can't do this!" she cries in the agony of childbirth.

She screams as the baby crowns.

"The baby's coming. Push!" the Doctor directs.

"You've got this. God has you!" her midwife cheers.

Next to her ear she hears her husband's gentle voice in earnest, his warm breath caressing her ear, "I love you. You're so beautiful."

Every role—all those who truly love you—is relevant and important in the birthing process of God's destiny for you. He loves you and whispers to your spirit, "You're so beautiful."

"I opened two gifts this morning. They were my eyes."

— UNKNOWN

One morning I woke up and all I could do was scream in pain. I literally couldn't open my right eye, and any needle point of light scorched it as tears streamed down my face. I was alone and terrified. I called my fiancé, begging him to come drive me to the hospital. As I waited in agony, I stood before the mirror trying to pry open the painful eye. I gasped when my good eye saw a person I did not recognize. Had I done something to deserve this?

As I strained at my reflection, a million thoughts raced through my head, and all I did in that moment was focus on the pain—and a little too long at the dreadful way I looked. I didn't pray. The moment I should have been praying the hardest, I was staring at myself and screaming in pain—pain that I wouldn't wish on anyone's enemy.

Once I arrived in the emergency room, the doctor called for an offsite corneal specialist. He was able to force my eye open and seemed startled at what he saw, like he was scared for me too.

Jesus, I cried from my heart, and finally my mind started to redirect to where my focus should have been from the beginning—on my Savior. God was the only one who could heal me. Jesus, I clutched in spirit. The doctor said I may lose my eye completely. Jesus, I reign in my fear. We are going to overcome this together.

From that firm decision within me, I refused to believe a diagnosis from just anyone, nor the comments of worried concern—although I knew they were well-meant. During that time, I developed a greater respect for people in the medical field. They had to do their jobs and they had to be realists. But even when I literally could not see, my faith required me to "live by faith, not by sight" (2 Corinthians 5:7).

Where there is no vision, the people perish: but he that keeps the law, happy is he.

— Proverbs 29:18

I had chosen to look at the situation from a new perspective. Even though my physical eyes were seemingly deteriorating, my spiritual eyes were becoming stronger than ever. Through my brokenness, Jesus kissed my forehead with His comfort and peace. Through my cries, I knew He was collecting my tears in a bottle to be turned into joy. Through my pain, He developed in me a greater understanding of my purpose. And through physical rest, I heard His voice so clearly that a new light of understanding dawned in me: I had always been made to believe that my eyes were my most beautiful attribute, but how could I have real empathy for what it means to be gorgeous inside unless I was tested on all levels?

It was in this season of new spiritual sight that I learned that the mirror is a faulty spectacle of who we really are. I learned to separate my inner self from my outer being like never before. Instead of sharing a "selfie," I saw that I had to work on my soul.

That season delayed a lot of things in my life. It almost stopped the publication of this book. In my mind, the book and my hopes were all too late. I had shared too much; people had stolen too much; the messages were too outdated . . . . These heavy thoughts that rolled through my head like a bowling ball were not of God. I realized I had to push through the birthing transition to overcome the final part of the birthing plan God had for my vision. It was time to push, and I knew in my heart I would be rewarded by Him.

> To the one who is victorious, I will give the right to
> sit with me on my throne, just as I was victorious
> and sat down with my Father on his throne.
>
> — REVELATION 3:21

> I have told you these things, so that in me you may
> have peace. In this world you will have trouble. But
> take heart! I have overcome the world.
>
> — JOHN 16:33

> For I am the LORD, your God, who takes hold of
> your right hand and says to you, Do not fear; I will
> help you.
>
> — ISAIAH 41:13

Absolutely nothing can stop God's calling on your life—except you.

When a woman is ready to push that baby from her womb, she couldn't care less about who's in the room, how busted up she looks, how annoying she may sound, or anything trifling. She couldn't care less how long the process has already taken and who tried to encourage her to abort early on, because she knows there's a calling on her life to birth something greater than her past and the pain. Pain doesn't eliminate purpose, it empowers it.

You see, each of us are pregnant in one way or another—full of ourselves or expectant with God's great purpose. We get to choose which direction we'll take. Birthing what He has planted in us requires patience, diligence, keen attention, and care throughout our entire spiritual pregnancies, unlike the selfie that just pops out at any given time.

There's something to learn at every single stage.

No matter where you are in your journey of life or how old you are, you are never "too" anything to dream big and walk out your God-ordained calling. Even though a woman's reproductive system expires through time, your spiritual purpose has absolutely no expiration date.

Do not abort. What's yours is yours. Women birth nations. We birth leaders. We birth purpose.

Wow! What a burden and responsibility—which is why every time you want to give up, it's key to remember *why* you're birthing your dream. If your why only leads to your own selfish desires, your 'baby' will never find its true beauty: to bless others and honor God.

There are some women reading this book right now who are called to be like Mary the mother of Jesus, to deliver a baby whose conception seems so unreal, and the development process, at times, so unbearable. Can you imagine what Mary was thinking when she was told that she would carry in her womb the King of Kings, Jesus? She was a virgin after all. Can you imagine the weight of holding such a purpose in her belly? Can you fathom the self-doubt and spiritual warfare she went through? You may not know the exact weight of Mary's cross, but you can relate because you're carrying your own purpose.

I've come to learn that trailblazers always go through an internal struggle: *can I do this? God, are You sure You want to use plain old me—the one with the broken past? The one who still struggles daily? The one who doesn't want to be seen? The one who feels she has nothing of value to offer? Are you sure it's me that You want to carry and birth this vision, Lord?*

If you've ever, for one second, had such thoughts and questions, I encourage you with a resounding YES! God wants to use those who have been discounted, neglected, broken—those who are pliable clay in His hands, to mold them into His vessels to carry very specific 'babies' into this world. He has already chosen *you* for an extraordinary purpose, but will you choose to follow Him? Will you choose to listen to the Doctor of your destiny? Will you muster the courage to overcome the battlefield of your mind? Our labor is never in vain, but there's always the possibility of pain. Are you bold enough carry the vision God has conceived in you, and do you have the courage to push? Push past the crowd, push past the unbelievers, push past the lies of the enemy, push past every taunting memory?

How?

When an angel of the Lord came to Mary and told her she would be pregnant with the Son of God, Mary asked, "How will this be . . . since I am a virgin" (Luke 1:34)?

The angel replied, 'The Holy Spirit will come on you, and the power of the Most High will overshadow you. So the holy one to be born will be called the Son of God. Even Elizabeth your relative is going to have a child in her old age, and she who was said to be unable to conceive is in her sixth month. For no word from God will ever fail" (Luke 1:35-37).

Mary responded "I am the Lord's servant . . . . May your word to me be fulfilled" (Luke 1:38).

How do you respond when God calls you do things for Him?

Mary's response left no room for doubt or fear because she fully trusted God. Goodness, I want to be like Mary! I'm sure after Mary's yes to God she still had moments of doubt, fear, and concern; after all, she was human like you and me. Mary gave God her yes and trusted Him to show her how to navigate in her own lane and how to be her own stepping stone. And He did not leave her alone on her pregnancy journey; He had shared with Mary that her relative Elizabeth would also be pregnant.

A few days later Mary greeted Elizabeth. At the sound of Mary's greeting, Elizabeth's baby "leaped in her womb, and Elizabeth was filled with the Holy Spirit" (Luke 1:41). She gave a glad cry and exclaimed to Mary, "Blessed are you among women, and blessed is the child you will bear! But why am I so favored, that the mother of my Lord should come to me? As soon as the sound of your greeting reached my ears, the baby in my womb leaped for joy. Blessed is she who has believed that the Lord would fulfill his promises to her" (Luke 1:42-45)!

Did you catch how Elizabeth didn't envy the nature of another woman's pregnancy? She knew that in Mary's belly was her God. She was hit so hard by that truth that the baby inside her *leaped*! Elizabeth's pregnancy would bear a different divine purpose from Mary's, so Elizabeth would need to stay in her own lane and be her own stepping stone. But she would not be alone on her journey. The delight and encouragement Mary had for Elizabeth's pregnancy walked with Elizabeth.

We don't have to bear our purposes alone! God strategically sends midwives and others in similar circumstances to walk with us and encourage us.

On the "Dedications" page at the beginning of this book, I referenced *My Midwives*. Why? Because as long and challenging it was for this 'baby' to be delivered, it would have been much more trying and lonely without their examples and enthusiasm. Merriam-Webster's dictionary references a midwife as "a person (usually a woman) who helps a woman when she is giving birth to a child."[1] A midwife keeps the mother focused on the ultimate goal and reminds her that she is strong enough to endure the entire process and be rewarded with the prize.

As we are always called to be like Mary in faith, we are also called to be an Elizabeth to others.

> *Countless times I closed my laptop in disobedience, thinking that there was one part or another in this book that I couldn't share with the world. Then, one sister of mine after another, being obedient to God, would encourage me to tread forward. They didn't know the full extent of the personal warfare I was going through—and they didn't need to know that—but they knew His voice and simply trusted and obeyed.*

What a beautiful God we serve who would call us to live out a part of His tapestry in design!

✑

If your answer to Christ, like Mary's, is YES, make sure your ears are so in tune with Jesus' voice that His words tune out the deceptively beautiful ballad of the enemy.

> *So many times I almost gave up. It was while writing this chapter that I raised my hand to Jesus for a voluntary C-section because I was tired from the labor to complete the birthing process of this book. Just cut it out of me, Lord, I cried. I can't take this heaviness and strain anymore! How do you want me to talk about birth when I've yet to bear a human child? Each time I grew weary and didn't want to push any longer, God would remind me that the push wasn't even about me— just like pushing a baby from a mother's womb is not about the mother. Pushing to birth God's*

vision is about new life in Christ that I have the privilege to share with others.

You too have that privilege.

---

[1] "midwife." *Merriam-Webster.com.* 2015. http://www.merriam-webster.com (21, February, 2016).

While they were there, the time came for the baby to be born.

— Luke 2:6

Are you going to push or are you going to let that baby (purpose) rot?

— Cecilia Simon

PUSH!

Chapter Twelve

GORGEOUS INSIDE: BIRTHING BASE, BALANCE, AND BEAUTY

How are your roots? I'm not asking about your latest hairdo, I'm asking about your inner base, balance, and beauty. When your world gets shaken, do you remain standing? What's a flashy building if it's bound to fall from lack of deep stability and balance when strong weather hits?

Base. Did you know that the taller a building is constructed, the deeper the construction team has to dig into the dirt? Yes, in order for a massive building to firmly withstand trembling winds, up-roaring floods, panicking shakes, and a stampede of people, the earth must first be broken and deeply dug, and the building's *base* must be rooted in solid ground.

Did you know that the depth of your past is an indication of the height of your future? As I check my own heart, I ask you, friend, are you building your dreams rooted in solid ground?

> Therefore everyone who hears these words of mine and puts them into practice is like a wise man who built his house on the rock. The rain came down, the

streams rose, and the winds blew and beat against that house; yet it did not fall, because it had its foundation on the rock.

— MATTHEW 7:24-25

Balance is the equally critical component in a building's construction, from its conception to blueprint to hard hats. Being gorgeous inside is also about balance. You cannot airbrush personality, copy depth, or crop substance. Don't become so absorbed with editing your outside that you completely neglect what's foundationally vital on the inside. Your outer being is just a shell. But who you are internally is what determines the *substance of your character*. Your spirit is eternal.

Beauty. We're all a work in progress. No two people are the same on the inside or out. But we all start with some kind of root system and balance, whether shallow or deep, wobbly or sturdy, from which either inner beauty or ugliness will grow outward. Outward beauty starts with the inner base and balance, and only you and God can see what's inside your spirit.

Likewise, you cannot see what's developing inside others. In relating to those around you, and in our human tendency to compare, don't be so caught up in how others appear from the outside that you totally discount what God is doing on their insides. Never be too serious to laugh, or too uppity to think you're too polished to benefit from more refining. Be teachable and pliable as the body is through pregnancy and birthing. A woman's body remembers the birthing path pioneered by the pressure it endured. Just as the rock undertook extreme pressure to become a diamond, just as the caterpillar had to endure the growing process to expand its vibrant wings, just as the crushing of olives produces healing, protective, preventive oil, and just as the pain and pressure of birth produces a healthy baby, God's anointing of your purpose often comes through the crushing of your spirit. Digging deep into the soil of your life and spirit will make way for a solid, balanced root system from which a solid, gorgeous inner person and outward purpose will grow. Do not deride the process and thereby your divine beauty and purpose, even though it will be painful at times. Your shine and the vision birthed from you will be worth all you've endured. For you did not overcome the pressures and pain without a divinely designed purpose. Be kind to others and yourself, and above all, honor God from within. These are *gorgeous* qualities.

> Let your light shine before others, that they may see
> your good deeds and glorify your Father in heaven.
> — Matthew 5:16

The transition stage of birthing your purpose means that you'll need be still when God leads you to be still, and push toward your mark when He says push. These factors are well beyond changing your feelings with the same ease as changing your clothes. Transition your concern about looking cute and impressing others to being healed, prepared, and empowered to boldly and beautifully walk the runway of your destiny. Push through to your divine destiny as a mother pushes her baby into the world. Push with no apprehension and push because someone else's life, or their eternity, may depend on your momentum.

> Seek meaning and appreciation in what has already been set aside uniquely and specifically for you. What God says is yours has no other name on it.

Finally, do not wish for someone else's portion. Though another's portion may, seemingly, look better to you from where you're sitting (or stuck), seek meaning and appreciation in what has already been set aside uniquely and specifically for you. What God says is *yours* has no other name on it. Embrace what is yours! Rejoice through all your seasons, for before you were born, you were set apart (Romans 12:2)! You are called to be a light in the darkness.

When you visit a jewelry store and ask to see a diamond, you may notice that the jeweler doesn't simply place the valuable stone on the counter's glass. The diamond is laid atop a dark-colored glass or cloth, positioned to best display the contrasts and shut out all distractions. The dark background makes the diamond pop and sparkle for your viewing pleasure. I pray that when anyone asks you about the nature of your spectacular glow against the darkness of this world, you'll give the glory to God. By doing so, you are allowing His Spirit to shine brightly through all the pressure and pain you've endured to become the gorgeous diamond you are.

You are so beautiful, inside and out. You are not your yesterdays and you are never "too" anything to start over. You do not have to conform to societal expectancies and your outer self is just a bonus.

His mercies (compassions) are "new every morning" for you (Lamentations 3:22-23)! Your inner spirit, where the glory of God dwells, is the core of your beauty. Refine and shine!

You are *gorgeous inside.*

THE GORGEOUS INSIDE CHALLENGE

Now that you've gained teaching and tips to encourage your refining, please take "The Gorgeous Inside Challenge" to encourage your sisters to refine and shine. I don't mean just the friends you find as you scroll through your contact list. Encourage strangers too—and make shining your light a daily habit. You never know who seriously needs a word of encouragement and reminder of God's love! How many times have you been having a bad day and felt blessed by a kind word or deed, right on time?! I dare say that rarely happens, but together we can change for good what the enemy set out to destroy: our gorgeous spirits!

HERE'S THE CHALLENGE:

How creative can you be to daily encourage the people God has placed on your path—including strangers? Beginning today, I encourage you to *get creative*. Let's start with . . .

The beauty of sticky notes and mini pens:

🌿 Leave a sticky note on a public restroom mirror—including your office and church, the convenience store bathroom you pop into, and the restaurant restrooms you frequent. Stick an encouraging note on the bathroom stall, and inside your restaurant bill holder, on car windows, on magazine tables at your doctor appointments, your hair appointments . . .

🌿 Your notes should remind others that the mirror will always be too fickle to reflect their true beauty. Or simply leave a word of encouragement! You can get as creative as you'd like! It's your *love note* to leave a little sprinkle of love for whoever finds it.

⮑ Sticky notes don't destroy property—like writing on the wall of the stall!

⮑ Sticky notes come in a vast array of colors and shapes.

⮑ Sticky notes and mini pens fit perfectly in your purse, even into the smallest handbag, the back pocket of your jeans, and your jacket.

⮑ Sticky notes and mini pens are inexpensive and available at most retail stores, even your local grocery.

What are *your* creative ideas? Post them at
www.WeAreGorgeousInside.com.

If you're on social media,
hashtag #WAGI #GorgeousInsideChallenge.

Let's cause a ripple effect for women *worldwide* as we share Christ's love with one another—one sticky note, one word, one prayer, one hug at a time!

Paloma Freeman was born in Lima, Peru and grew up in Northern Virginia with her mother and large extended family. She would describe herself as out of the box; a mix of introvert and extrovert depending on the season. She enjoys talking to strangers and reminding women where their true beauty stems from.

She graduated from Lynn University with a bachelor in Criminal Justice and psychology. She is a full time Wellness Coach and Quit Coach, helping people break addictions and walk in their full potential. She shares that her tranquility comes from quiet moments, books, prayer for others, nature, and pouring her heart on to pages as Jesus holds the pen.

> My heart is stirred by a noble theme
> as I recite my verses for the king;
> my tongue is the pen of a skillful writer.
>
> — PSALM 45:1

She currently resides in Florida with her husband and has launched a ministry for women entitled 'We Are Gorgeous Inside' for women who've struggled with confidence, finding Christ, and walking in His freedom.

www.WeAreGorgeousInside.com   #WAGI #GorgeousInsideChallenge.